THE PERSON I AM

THE PERSON I AM

Glenn H. Asquith

ABINGDON PRESS

Nashville
New York

THE PERSON I AM

Copyright © 1969 by Abingdon Press

All rights in this book are reserved. No part of the book may be reproduced in any manner whatsoever without written permission of the publishers except brief quotations embodied in critical articles or reviews. For information address Abingdon Press, Nashville, Tennessee.

Standard Book Number: 687-30769-4

Library of Congress Catalog Card Number: 69-18449

Scripture quotations noted RSV are from the Revised Standard Version of the Bible, copyrighted 1946 and 1952 by the Division of Christian Education, National Council of Churches, and are used by permission.

SET UP, PRINTED, AND BOUND BY THE PARTHENON PRESS, AT NASHVILLE, TENNESSEE, UNITED STATES OF AMERICA

Dedicated to my wife's father
Americus R. Underdown, Jr.
and to the memory of her mother
Anna T. Underdown

Preface

"Who am I?"

This question fairly shouted at me from the pages of a book I was about to discard. The volume was one of a number of uncertain vintage that I had acquired or inherited over the years. It had been published in 1908 as an authority in a field that had changed drastically since the author had put down "the last word" on his particular subject. But even though I considered that this book had no further relevance to my work or world, I opened it here and there at random and was startled to read:

"The vital question before us now is, 'Who am I?'"

To say the least that deserved to be said, this was a most surprising observation to have been made at the turn of the century inasmuch as recent thinkers and writers were assuring the public that they had stumbled upon and were in possession of a fresh approach to life: inquire often and long, "Who am I"!

Further thought, however, brought to mind that this concern is far older than 1908. In ancient times Greek philosophers advised their pupils: "Know thyself."

Of far greater significance than this is the constant instruction of the New Testament that everyone take heed to himself and be aware of the kind of person he is.

Even so, the many wise men who have left the prescription for honest self-study are forgotten in the daily rush of life with its many demands and concerns; there seems little available time to pause and wonder, "Who am I?"

To the many blessings of late maturity may be added the opportunity for getting acquainted with oneself.

This book endeavors to lead the reader into the rich experience of coming to know, as never before, that remarkable—yes, wonderful—person who is himself.

GLENN H. ASQUITH

Contents

The Person Inside

Mysterious 17
Self-Assessed 20
Compared to Others 23
Hypocritical 26
Exposed to God 29
Fearful 32
Prone to Sin 35
Indestructible 38
The Lost Is Found 41
The Great Amen 44

The Person Outside

Temple of God	49
Thing of Beauty	52
Sacrifice	55
Soul's Battleground	58
Place of Hunger	61
Cage of Anxieties	64
Source of Imaginations	67
In the Especial Care of God	70
Sheltered	73
Mind-Nourished	76

The Person with Persons

Desert Island for Sale	81
Part of a Whole	84
In a Home	87
Link in a Chain	90
Doing with Others	93
Feelings Shared	96
One Body	99
Hearing Together	102
Loneliness Unnecessary	105
Lovely Mosaic	108

The Person Eternal

Life Exciting, Except—	113
"I Am Fine"	116
"If a Man Die"	119
What Shall We Have?	122
Things Abandoned	125
Life—a Reward	128
Safe in God's Hands	131
The Heavenly Bank	134
Life—the First Qualification	137
There Is No Death	140
Conclusions	143

The Person Inside

Mysterious

"And he asked him, What is thy name? And he answered, saying, My name is Legion: for we are many." (Mark 5:9)

"Who will speak to my condition?" pleaded George Fox. He took this question up and down the highways of England, into churches and chapels, into homes and public places. He wanted something that would satisfy his inner person. In disappointment he found that no one had anything to offer for his particular need. In an endeavor to solve his problem, he started something which grew into the Society of Friends—later dubbed the Quaker movement.

This same condition of inner unrest was felt by a man past sixty who had suffered a slight heart attack. He did not make as rapid a recovery as he had hoped, and he grew increasingly concerned. Finally, his doctor pinpointed the trouble, and said, "You are a very complicated person; if you were a simple soul I could get you out of this much faster."

But who is a simple soul? George Fox and the troublesome patient are fair samples of what we are—all of us. The person inside is a mysterious and many-sided person. We, too, can call our name Legion because we are many. And this may well explain why we have frequent periods of disquiet when we cannot describe what is wrong: We are not hungry, thirsty, angry, worried, or persecuted. Seemingly, for no reason at all, the inner person is ill at ease. Who can speak to this condition when we ourselves do not know what the condition is?

Indeed, that ageless person inside is mysterious and many-sided. This is bound to be true inasmuch as we have something of the image of God in us. In one of the holy books of India is a story of a man who prayed to see God in his completeness. His request was granted, but the sight afforded him was so awesome that he had to cry, "No more!" For God was seen as so truly infinite, so much involved in everything that he had created, so able to do all things that no man could take in more than a tiny bit of the divine whole.

However, knowing that the person inside *is* complex is a beginning of new understanding about ourselves. No longer need we be dismayed that we have strange and haunting yearnings when music is played, when the world speaks to us in springtime, or when in some other way we become aware of something beyond our day-to-day routine.

Read about a man who was puzzled about himself: Rom. 7:19-25.

Prayer: My Father, help me toward the first efforts in self-exploration. Amen.

Self-Assessed

"He is like unto a man beholding his natural face in a glass; for he beholdeth himself, and goeth his way, and straightway forgetteth what manner of man he was." (Jas. 1:23-24)

"Mirror, mirror on the wall—"

As children, how we enjoyed that fairy tale in which the far-from-pretty queen wanted to be told that she was the fairest one of all, when we knew that there was a girl in the story who was the true beauty!

In real life, however, we may not be so unlike the queen as we take a look at the person inside fully expecting that we shall find him superior in every way!

The reason for this may be, partly, that others have been too kind and complimentary—our friends, for instance.

Friends say such nice things about us! How talented we are, how we do not show our age, how witty and interesting is our conversation! Indeed, friends make a wonderful mirror—we look in that glass and are certain that we have seen our real selves.

And then articles in magazines tell us how important we are and what tremendous potentialities we have realized. The writers hold out before us a fascinating future in which we are to remember great exploits and enjoy the rightful fruits of notable endeavors. Here again, we find a satisfying mirror when we are seeking to know ourselves.

Doctors also often prove to be a third source of comfort. We may go to them with fear and uncertainty about our aches and pains and the years that have accumulated so quickly. Our physician assures us that we are vigorous and have years of joy ahead. This mirror we gaze in with lingering delight.

In fact, we go from mirror to mirror that we would gladly believe as we try earnestly to find that inner person, but as soon as we are alone we realize that friends, writers, doctors, and others are not showing us the whole picture. That person within is far more than anything we have found, and deserves a closer scrutiny than that of well-meaning acquaintances and strangers.

In the "stillness of the night" when the darkness makes all mirrors useless, what do we think of the person inside?

Look at one who assessed himself: Judg. 16:20.

Prayer: Forgive my stumbling search for truth, O Lord, and lead me on the way to find the self akin to thee. Amen.

Compared to Others

"For we dare not make ourselves of the number, or compare ourselves with some that commend themselves: but they measuring themselves by themselves, and comparing themselves among themselves, are not wise." (II Cor. 10:12)

"Four eyes!" "Tenderfoot!" the North Dakota ranchers taunted the bespectacled, educated, and seemingly little man from the "East." They were comparing themselves with Theodore Roosevelt. According to their rugged notions of what constituted a "man" this newcomer was not a man.

And Roosevelt accepted their challenge and set out to prove that he could shoot, fight, ride long hours in the saddle, and in every way hold his own with the best of them.

This future President of the United States was doing what all of us have done so often—he was conforming to the standards where he found himself. Even when we are dealing with the person inside, it seems adequate to be able to say, "I am as good as he is!" or "I am not so bad as she is!"

When we think soberly about this kind of measuring of ourselves we know that it is not accurate, to say the least. But it becomes tragic if carried to an evaluation of the person inside. That person is unique and has an individual purpose and destiny not to be found true of the inner being of anyone else. What if a thoroughbred horse were satisfied to amble along at a speed only as great as that of a farm horse pulling a load? Or what if a work mare were condemned simply because she could not run as fast as the racehorse? Each is gifted and intended for a special task.

Roosevelt, of course, knew this. He soon departed from the life of the western rancher and went back to Washington to use his heritage and training and talents in the service of mankind and his country.

But if we cannot find among ourselves others with whom the inner person may be compared, how shall we go forward in our search for self-knowledge?

Will not the answer be that we are to go back to the Source year after year and compare the inner person with the Creator? Otherwise our experience may be like that of a man who had a duplicate key made for his front door and found it did not turn the lock. The trouble was that the new key had been copied from a copy of a copy, and not from the original; exactness had been lost.

Looking at the specifications: Eph. 4:13

Prayer: Show me thyself, O Lord. Amen.

Hypocritical

"Moreover, when ye fast, be not, as the hypocrites, of a sad counterance: for they disfigure their faces, that they may appear unto men to fast." (Matt. 6:16)

The doorbell rang, and, when the woman of the house came to see who the caller might be, she found a small figure on the step, dressed in a rabbit suit. The long ears, cotton-ball tail, and white stomach made it quite clear that this Hallowe'en visitor was a bunny. However, without thinking the woman exclaimed, "How cute you are, Billy Brown!" A muffled and indignant voice replied, "I am not Billy Brown, I am a rabbit."

Here was a clear case of hypocrisy! A small boy pretending to be a rabbit! An innocent and amusing trick, but an illustration of how anyone can be so taken up by a false identity that he more than halfway believes in the fraud.

Even with the person inside we indulge in hypocrisy. There is little doubt that men such as Hitler and Napoleon have believed themselves to be the opposite of what history has proved them to be. On the other side, it is entirely possible for seemingly saintly people to be positive that they are the world's worst sinners.

All of this comes about in the struggle to examine the inner person and to know him for what he is. So often he becomes to us what we desperately want him to be rather than what we have made of him.

The very fact, however, that we are willing to seek out what we really are is a blessing in itself and can prove to be the most helpful thing that could happen to us. Mentally we may follow the example of a young man who had fallen deeply into debt because of expensive tastes and failure to realize his financial limitations, and who kept putting off a much-needed examination of his circumstances. He paid only the creditors who demanded something on account. This way of life kept him in misery and uncertainty. Finally, he decided to face up to the situation. He purchased a small cashbook, and wrote down what he owed and to whom. Then he budgeted his income and paid something on each bill every payday. His mind was eased, and he was on his way to a true understanding of his position at all times.

Something of this kind can happen to us in our maturity as we become acquainted with the true dimensions of the person inside. We can see our masks and rip them off.

One who knew the folly of hypocrisy: Job 27:8-11.

Prayer: Heavenly Father, help me to be true and sincere and without pretense in thy sight. Amen.

Exposed to God

"But Jesus did not commit himself unto them, because he knew all men, and needed not that any should testify of man: for he knew what was in man." (John 2:24-25)

"I can't wait to see what comes up!" exclaimed an eight-year-old boy who was helping his father develop some pictures. They were in a darkroom that they had made in the basement. The lad had taken some snapshots, but when he had seen the negatives he could not make out what the contrasts of black and white meant. His father had told him, "We will have to expose these to a strong light and then put the print paper in a tray with some developer fluid." Bending over this tray the boy watched as there appeared the dim outlines of what would be soon a finished picture.

In our search for the person inside we have scrutinized the "negatives" that others have taken of us, or that we have been able to produce, and our knowledge of ourselves is still partial and faulty. Not until we are fully exposed to God can we hope to have an understandable image of what and who we are. There is something so exciting about realizing that there is One who can show us our true selves that we at our age may be as eager as the boy in the darkroom: what is going to come up?

And unlike any probing person or agency in our immediate world, the Lord will not refer us here, there, and the other place to "specialists." He knows us in every part just as a craftsman who has made a product by hand knows everything that has gone into it. He looks at us from a base of knowledge and not as though he were exploring some new thing. With this in mind we can expose ourselves to God in great confidence, for he will not be surprised by what we are. He knows full well what we are, and he knows how we have marred the original creation as well as how we have added to its worth. The effects of our many years are open to him.

However, if we are not comforted or satisfied by what others have said of us in answer to our question, "Who am I?" and decide to go all the way in discovering our true selves, we must be prepared to accept "what comes up" when we expose ourselves to God. But the venture will be so worthwhile! And how we will be inspired to bring everything into keeping with the best that "comes up"!

God's knowledge of the person inside: Ps. 139: 1-16.

Prayer: I continue, O Lord, in my hunt for the true person inside, as I hesitantly expose myself to thy searching eye. Amen.

Fearful

"And he saith unto them, Why are ye fearful, O ye of little faith?" (Matt. 8:26)

A catalog of fears! Who has one? But if there were such a catalog, even one as huge as that thick mail-order book that was familiar in our childhood, it would be difficult for most of us to find one listed fear that we have not experienced at one time or another. Fears for our aging selves: sickness, incapacity, insecurity, loneliness, failure, injury, pain, saying or doing the wrong thing. Fears for family: misbehavior, disgrace, disease, ingratitude, death, lack of opportunity. Fears for the world: war, natural disaster, economic ruin, "ism's," immorality. Particular fears and general fears and ungrounded fears keep us in *such* a turmoil! God knows this about us.

And these fears are something like a roadblock placed in the way of health. The issues of life may back up against this dam or roadblock until the wholesome freshness of our bodies and minds is replaced by stagnancy and dark depths. New channels for service and love cannot be cut since our streams of faith and high purpose are not free to move out and on.

In the exposure of our inner person God will show us that our fears are for the most part without a reason. They are much like the fear of a man who was traveling at night on a train. He had read that red lights appear along the track when there is danger ahead, and the engineer knows that he must stop. Looking through the window as the train roared along, this passenger was terrified to see a red light passed without the train being slowed down at all. He ran to the conductor and told him what the engineer had failed to do. But the conductor explained: "When we came to that light it was green to show us the way was clear;

when the engine passed the light it turned red to protect us from any train following too closely behind us."

In this same apprehensive mood we fear the needle that will give us a life-saving injection; we fear strange places that are to be to us much better than the old and familiar; we walk in dread of catastrophes that never happen.

We shall make progress in our search for the true person inside if we admit that we are fearful and accept this fact as part of the picture that is coming clear as we look at ourselves with honesty.

What to do with fear: Luke 12:4-7.

Prayer: Lord, may I learn day by day to place my fears before thee, trusting that thou art able to dispel them. Amen.

Prone to Sin

"For I know that in me (that is, in my flesh,) dwelleth no good thing: for to will is present with me; but how to perform that which is good I find not. For the good that I would I do not: but the evil which I would not, that I do." (Rom. 7:18-19)

"Gigo!" said the computer operator, as he looked ruefully at the answers from his machine.

"What do you mean by that?" asked a bystander.

"Oh, it's an expression we use; *gigo*—garbage in, garbage out. If we do not program this thing correctly, if we put in the wrong information, we get what I have here: worthless results.

This was the principle accepted by some of the people in Jesus' day, and they had minute laws concerning their food and the washing of hands. Our Lord pointed out that it is not what goes into a man but what comes out that makes for sin or righteousness. And yet many of us—in fact, all of us—fall into the clutches of gigo. If we are mistreated we give our adversary "as good as he sent." This results in broken friendships, divorce, splits in churches, ill health, and war in the world. As we look deeply into the person inside we shall need to admit that he is prone to sin.

And when we sin we deliver ourselves into the hands of sin and are used for purposes far beneath those intended for us by the Creator God.

Like the marble in Vermont, for instance. A traveler was amazed to find a pigsty made of pure marble. He questioned the farmer as to why this valuable stone was used for such a common purpose? The reply was that the marble was handy and was not doing anyone any good, so it was appropriated.

When we return to the world just what the

world puts into us, we become available for unworthy uses.

However, even though we find that we are prone to sin, we shall learn about ourselves also that the person inside is struggling terrifically to do good and break away from the "garbage-in-garbage-out" temptation. Life has brought to us so much of injury, injustice, ingratitude that it is easy now to flare up and do unto others as they have done unto us. Always the person inside has the help of God to win the victory.

A rescued sinful man: Luke 22:31-32.

Prayer: Lord, I feel that knowing my weakness has helped me to watch my words and my deeds; give me strength in time of temptation. Amen.

Indestructible

"Unto the upright there ariseth light in the darkness: he is gracious, and full of compassion, and righteous. . . . Surely he shall not be moved for ever: the righteous shall be in everlasting remembrance." (Ps. 112:4-6)

The amusing remark of a little girl when she noticed her skin peeling from a sunburn, "I am only four years old, and I'm wearing out already!" has its sobering side. Without being morbid we recognize that aging parts of us wear out.

Indeed, we learned in school that in some ways we are new people every seven years because of the replacement of cells. Perhaps God created us as automobiles are said to be made: with built-in obsolescence.

And yet there is something different about the person inside. Some pessimistic writers would have us believe that we are like the "one-hoss shay" in the old poem .When the maker of this vehicle set about his task, he searched for materials with the same wearing qualities. And the poem tells us that the "shay" lasted exactly one hundred years. On the very anniversary of the construction of this remarkable little carriage it collapsed, and nothing was left but a pile of dust: Everything had worn out completely at the same time!

As we expose ourselves to God we find that this is not true of us. There is an indestructible part that will be left when everything else has served its day. We find that that inner person is more like a diamond than like the one-hoss shay. When the perishable setting falls away, the diamond remains. And the inner person is like the gems that are in the miner's pan after the earth and sand are washed away; and like the pure gold that appears when fire has consumed the dross.

Once we have established the fact of our indestructibility—since God has shown us our permanency—we find new meanings to the other facts we have discovered about the person inside. If we are hypocritical, sinful, fearful, these failings impinge on eternity; if we are joyful, radiant, loyal and faithful, these, also, have a shade of the everlasting.

A snowman, for instance, may be made carelessly; it will soon melt away. But a figure of marble or bronze must be carved with the utmost care; it will last indefinitely.

The promise of God's remembrance: Rev. 3:5.

Prayer: May I realize the meaning of my endless destiny and take heart and hope, O God. Amen.

The Lost Is Found

"For this my son was dead, and is alive again; he was lost, and is found." (Luke 15:24)

"The good old days!" is an expression we use (and too often!) that has become unpopular with younger people. We are told to remember that in the good old days people had a shorter life expectancy; many of the new inventions and conveniences such as television, jet air travel, cheap automobiles, automation of many kinds were not fully developed. But are we thinking of these material things when we have a homesickness for the past? Or are we thinking of what we were then?

Perhaps the person inside makes any day—past or present—good or ill.

By harking back to the good old days we may be following the example of detectives who try to reconstruct the scene and events of a crime. Only with us we are trying to recover a blessedness, not a crime. In order to find the real inner person we retrace in memory the long road of the years until we come to the spot where that person was at his best. That spot may have been in early childhood, in adolescence, in young manhood or womanhood; it may have been the moment when we were most conscious of surrendering to God; it may have been an hour of deep devotion to some person or cause.

In a sense this is what psychiatrists do with their patients. The physician leads the patient back, back, back—even to early childhood if necessary—until the point is discovered where the person began to depart from a normal life of love and security. Then the patient is guided to start from that point as though he were growing up again, and to take up life with that "found" self.

And what a wonderful experience it is when we

know that the real person inside is "found"! The woes of having lost the real self for awhile soon grow dim, and we exult in knowing what we are in spirit and in truth. God guides us to this as no doctor in this world can do. When we are lost the Father finds us, sometimes hidden deep "among the stuff" of this harried world.

Rejoicing over the found: Luke 15:3-7.

Prayer: My Heavenly Father, may the person inside be found just as were the lost sheep, the lost coin, and the lost son. Keep me from growing discouraged as I look diligently for the precious self that I may have mislaid in my headlong career through life. Amen.

The Great Amen

"Blessed be the Lord for evermore. Amen, and Amen. (Ps. 89:52)

More than a century ago Adelaide Proctor wrote:

> Seated one day at the Organ,
>   I was weary and ill at ease,
> And my fingers wandered idly
>   Over the noisy keys.
>
> I know not what I was playing,
>   Or what I was dreaming then;
> But I struck one chord of music,
>   Like the sound of a great Amen.

These verses describe, somewhat, the search we have been making for the person inside. We have found many noisy keys on the organ of life, but we have been looking for "The Lost Chord." And now as we find it, the satisfaction and glow will be like hearing a great Amen.

We need to hear that Amen, that Yes to our questions. What is life? Why am I here? Has it been worth it? Finding the real person inside will bring a final affirmation of what we have been doing in the world, and what we are to be in the future. "Maybes," "perhapses," "buts," and "ifs" leave us frightened and uncertain. The inner person is a permanent and solid part of God's plan and purpose, and when we discover this how different the days become!

Possibly not many of us still have the keenness of memory to recall the day when we first walked sturdily on our own two feet. But we can recapture this experience by watching toddlers of today. How wobbly and unsure are the first steps! But then the child gets the feel of it and strides out with confidence. That has been our experience, too. In times of doubt, pain, loss, grief, or coming disability we have found that the inner person eventually gets the feel of it and can walk through joy or sorrow with equal poise and assurance. The great Amen comes from deep in our being, and we know that we have been made and prepared by our Creator to get the best of all circumstances.

Who then is my person inside? Of all his characteristics the quality of being the great Amen to life is the capstone that sums up the rest.

A man of the long ago who heard his great Amen: Phil. 4:11-13.

Prayer: Lord, may I exult in the finality of my being. May I know that there is within me not "yes" and "no," but a firm "yes" answering life's problems. Amen.

The Person Outside

Temple of God

"Know ye not that ye are the temple of God, and that the Spirit of God dwelleth in you? If any man defile the temple of God, him shall God destroy; for the temple of God is holy, which temple ye are." (I Cor. 3:16-17)

As much as two thirds of our life, so insist some statisticians, is used upon the body: feeding it, resting it, exercising it, dressing and washing and grooming it, working to make money to provide its necessities. This accumulated investment of time surely justifies our consideration of the person outside.

The body, the soul—our physical nature, our

spiritual nature. These terms we use for want of better as we turn our quest for understanding from the person inside to the person outside. And it is our frequent temptation to consider the body outside as inferior to the supposedly "more spiritual" person on the inside. Perhaps as we learn how interdependent the two are, we shall raise our estimate of that part of the whole individual that the world calls "us."

Certainly the changing body will take on more dignity if we recognize it as having a divine inhabitant. Wherever the Spirit of God is, that dwelling place becomes a temple.

The fact of the body being a temple for God may be understood if we observe how the rough shell of the oyster is essential for holding a pearl. Or how the case of a watch is necessary to contain the "works." Or how an ungainly safe is the repository for priceless treasure. We are so created that there can be no person inside without the person outside.

Once in a great while the person outside gives a hint of the Spirit within. Phillips Brooks noted that in the story of the Transfiguration, Jesus' body shone and he stood before the disciples glistering and glorious. From this account Brooks concluded that at times "the body shares the gladness of the soul." And some have said that by looking at the first disciples they could tell that they had "been with Jesus." Usually, however, the person outside (much like the ridged oyster shell or the bunglesome safe) keeps to itself the secret of the unseen glory within. We need then to remind ourselves often that we are temples.

One who referred to the body temple: John 2:18-21.

Prayer: O Heavenly Father, as I feel the pull of the body with its demands and its urges may I be patient but firm in my answers to it. Amen.

Thing of Beauty

"I will praise thee; for I am fearfully and wonderfully made: marvelous are thy works; and that my soul knoweth right well." (Ps. 139:14)

"I surely wouldn't win a beauty contest!" Who has not said that at one time or another—particularly after youth has left us? But what kind of contest do we mean?

If we are thinking of a Miss America, Mr. America, Miss Universe, or Mr. World tryout, then we could be quite right in our pessimistic view of our bodies. These events have certain standards of beauty that we do not measure up to. If, however, there were contests for the kind of beauty that only artists see, it is more than likely that each of us could win something.

A walk through the average art gallery will prove that artists have taken the human body as the subject of more of their works than anything else in the world. And the models include mature people, elderly people, people with physical flaws and disproportions. This would seem to prove that years show beauty in different ways and in much variety.

Perhaps this can best be explained by knowing that there is about the human body a mysterious quality that speaks of the image of God. Even though God is spirit, he created us in such a way that we illustrate his being. Painters and sculptors have recognized this in their search for that which is beyond this earth.

Indeed, we might think of our person outside as growing into true beauty just as a statue is more and more lovely as the sculptor shapes it day by day until it is finished. And even after the chisel is laid aside, the statue has not acquired its ultimate beauty. It must take on what is called the "patina." This is a softening and mellowing of the surface that only exposure to the air for years can bring. Childhood and youth have "prettiness," but maturity only can come to authentic beauty. Years of love, suffering, struggling, learning, and being involved in all aspects of living put on the patina that is the finishing touch to beauty. Curves, freshness of skin, and sparkling eyes may not be our chief distinguishing marks now, but we have the angles and planes and etching lines that were missing in the beginning beauty of our youth.

God's standard of beauty: I Sam. 16:7.

Prayer: Let me not despise my appearance or the appearance of my companions, O Lord, but may I see beauty as thou dost see it. Amen.

Sacrifice

"*I beseech you therefore, brethren, by the mercies of God, that ye present your bodies a living sacrifice, holy, acceptable unto God, which is your reasonable service.*" *(Rom. 12:1)*

"Reserved for the King!" Some such sign as this was attached to the tallest, the straightest, and the best oaks in the English colonies of the New World. A settler in what is now New Jersey, for instance, could cut any trees on his land except those that had been selected as future masts for the King's navy. These would die by the ax that sailors might be carried safely across stormy seas.

Our person outside is in the same circumstances

as the marked tree. It is a sacrifice that must be given for the service of God. Sometimes the body dies as a whole sacrifice at one time as did the young man in Dicken's *Tale of Two Cities.* Sydney Carton takes the place of Charles Darnay in a cell during the French Revolution and dies on the guillotine in his stead. Usually, however, the body does not die quickly; more often the sacrifice is gradual. A mother cares for little children in the home and denies her body the fun and finery it might have otherwise; others care for the aged; for forty to fifty years men go out to a worthwhile daily job that will add to the life of mankind. The apostle Paul said, "I die daily" (I Cor. 15:31).

And what of Hannah in the Old Testament? Did she not give her person outside as a sacrifice when she took her long-desired child, Samuel, to serve in God's house? She denied herself love and care in her coming old age, she made the garments for her son, and trudged to the holy place with them yearly. Every day she died a little.

As we look at the person outside as a sacrifice we have a comfort in knowing that we are acceptable. In ancient times sacrificial animals or other offerings had to be perfect and without blemish or they were not worthy of the altar. But no matter how misshapen, old, stiff, scarred or awkward the human body may be it is holy and right for sacrifice if the heart is willing to give it. It becomes perfect in the eyes of God.

Another, and solemn, thought of the body as sacrifice comes from remembrance of the Last Supper that Jesus ate with his disciples before going to the cross: he spoke of giving his body for them.

What dignity the person outside begins to take on!

One whose person outside was offered: II Tim. 4:6-8.

Prayer: Here is my body, Lord. May it be given for thee. Amen.

Soul's Battleground

"But I keep under my body, and bring it into subjection: lest that by any means, when I have preached to others, I myself should be a castaway." (I Cor. 9:27)

"We have met the enemy, and he is us!" said a comic strip character. How very true we find this! The body is a chief battleground of the soul.

Sometimes we speak of a man or woman as being at the "dangerous age." Family reared, job conquered, financial security no longer calling for day and night attention, perhaps retirement, and then—time on his or her hands! Time to think of what has been missed in life; idle hours to be filled.

So often the soul warfare becomes acute as later years come on.

Hymn writers have been aware of this personal struggle:

> "Fight the good fight with all thy might!"
> "Sure I must fight if I would win."
> "Onward, Christian soldiers!"
> "Yield not to temptation."
> "Foes without, and foes within."

As we sing, do we recognize how much of this turmoil is caused by the person outside?

Unhappily, or happily perhaps, no one of us is an exception. The philosopher Nietzsche spoke scornfully of some people who boasted of their goodness. He said they were like a lion with lame paws. He could not fight and he could not hunt down his prey so he had to be tame and good. Nietzsche hinted that these "good" people were so weak, poor, unimportant, and ignorant that they had no choice but to be good. How wrong he was! Anyone, no matter what his physical, financial, or social position, has a terrific battle going on with his body.

The Persians spoke of this combat as between light and dark. Light is always in danger of being shadowed or eclipsed by darkness. Almost always there is the willing spirit, but the weak flesh.

A test as to how we are making out in the long campaign is to ascertain which is better fed—soul or body? Which is in a state of discipline? Which is the means of life, and which is the end?

We can be sure that the body will never give up until the last day of life; it is a stubborn foe!

Some words of a warrior: Rom. 6:6.

Prayer: Give me the victory, Lord, as hourly I am tempted and taunted by this body of mine. Amen.

Place of Hunger

"But he answered and said, It is written, Man shall not live by bread alone, but by every word that proceedeth out of the mouth of God." (Matt. 4:4)

A television crew went to the campus of a New York university to report a student demonstration against some action of the school officials. The pictures they took showed the young men and women in possession of the Administration Building: they were peering from all windows, clinging to the walls, and climbing from stone to stone. This could be an illustration of the unruliness of the hungers of the person outside. The person inside refuses to honor a carnal desire, and immediately he is besieged on all sides by the cravings and appetites of the physical being.

Those of us who may have been placed on a bland diet know how hard it is to resist the bodily demand for hearty food! Often the temptation is so strong that it seems that the delicious piece of dessert on the table must be eaten no matter what the cost in health!

And many who have tried to stop smoking have testified to the fierceness of the battle between what the nerves cry for and the right course of action.

Another hunger is that for intimacies which may either enrich marriage or result in broken homes and ruined lives.

It is no disgrace that the person outside presents us with wants for satisfaction of many kinds: All these desires are based on God's design for health, joy, and the continuance of the race. Food, drink, mating, rest, change of pace are built-in hungers to keep us alive and fit. But when one or more of the appetites assumes command of the whole person, finer things die. We live by so much more than these physical needs.

Even a casual scrutiny of present-day advertisements will show that they are written and illustrated to appeal to the longings of the person outside: "Treat yourself" to this or that; "reward yourself" with one thing or another; "don't worry about overeating or overdrinking" so long as you have this fizzy tablet to take afterward.

Many years ago a man thought of appetite and reason as being like two buckets on an old well chain: When one was up the other was down, and the man said he was happiest when the "reason bucket" was uppermost.

A question about the person outside: Phil. 3:20-21.

Prayer: O Lord, may the hungers of my body always be my friends and not my enemies. Amen.

Cage of Anxieties

"But the Lord answered her, 'Martha, Martha, you are anxious and troubled about many things; one thing is needful.'" (Luke 10:41-42 RSV)

In a story a young woman had been told that she was suffering from an incurable disease and had about six months to live. Immediately she began to be anxious that she would miss many things in life that she had never experienced. So she sold everything she had, took the money, went to a gay city, and began to "live it up." Luxuries, good food, excitement, interesting companions, trips to places of interest filled her days.

Something of this same feeling must have

moved the Prodigal Son (Luke 15) to take his share of the farm in cash and go to a far country: He was anxious about being stuck off in the country where nothing would ever happen to him.

The person outside often is a cage of anxieties, fearing many things. Will there be food to eat? Will there be something to drink? These clothes are old, where shall I get new ones? I may get hurt, I may die, my children may get in trouble, my income or my pension may be reduced. No lion tamer shut in with wild animals has a rougher crew to deal with than these anxieties.

Perhaps the greatest drawback that cares present is that they they consume time that could be spent to better advantage. Apparently Martha wanted the next meal to turn out just right! She was concerned that her guests have every courtesy and comfort. The house must be spick-and-span. But these anxieties kept her from talking to the Lord of life. She stayed in the cage to tame them instead of going out and locking the door behind her.

Just as with hungers, however, we may need to admit that some anxieties are wholesome. Psychologists have said that tension of itself is not a killing factor in life—in fact, there must be a certain amount of tension to guarantee escape from danger and to prod one to achievement. Fatal tensions are those that push faith out.

This fanciful story of a bishop may help our thinking. This worthy, elderly churchman knelt down to say his evening prayers and then got into bed and tossed and turned with worry. A voice came: "Bishop, why not go to sleep? I, your God, may be able to take care of the world until morning!"

What to do with anxieties: Matt. 6:25-34.

Prayer: May I practice casting my cares upon thee, O loving Father. Amen.

Source of Imaginations

"And it shall come to pass afterward, that I will pour out my spirit upon all flesh; and your sons and your daughters shall prophesy, your old men shall dream dreams, your young men shall see visions." (Joel 2:28)

"Oh, you are just imagining things!" we say to a child who insists that there is a tiger in the back yard. And of course that child and all children—and their fathers and mothers and grandfathers and grandmothers all the way back to Adam and Eve—have imagined things. The world is an exciting place due to our imaginations. We "image" things in our minds and see better things or worse things, new things or ancient things.

And the person outside—the body—has much to do with the quality of the imaginations. If undisciplined and given authority, the outside person controls the images just about as a thermostat controls the temperature of a house. Hunger, fatigue, depression, joy of movement, quietness, and energy all raise or lower the standard of imagination. As the years press in on us, we need to keep this firmly in mind.

Adolf Hitler, the German dictator, in the terrible years of 1939-45, moved an entire nation to follow his imaginations of a "super race" ruling the world. Doctors and psychologists, who have pondered on the evidence of what this man was, think there is ample reason to believe that Hitler's physical condition had much to do with his outlook on the world.

On the other hand, Abram could see a city of God ahead of him across the weary miles of wilderness, and the founding fathers of the United States of America saw a nation governed on the principle of equality and opportunity for all men. Perhaps they kept their bodies under orders so that they were keenly receptive to the promptings of God.

Does this line of thought bring a new light on the desirability for maintaining the best physical fitness that our circumstances and makeup permit? The person outside needs to be taken into account, not only for the purposes of getting us around, making it possible for us to serve in some way and find enjoyment, but as a powerful source of imagination for good.

It may have been that Shakespeare was thinking of imagination when he said that we are "spies for God." What is there in our neighbor that ought to be encouraged? What potential is there in our world that could come into being? By the spirit of the Lord, how the images come flocking!

Paul speaks of imaginations: II Cor. 10:1-5.

Prayer: May the images that form in my mind, O God, be in accord with thy will. Amen.

In the Especial Care of God

"What is man, that thou art mindful of him? and the son of man, that thou visitest him?" (Ps. 8:4)

"TLC" is an expression used by nurses meaning "tender, loving care." There are patients—particularly boys and girls in the children's ward—that need TLC more than medicine or surgery. And which of us ever outgrows that need?

This need becomes more pronounced if anything as we grow older and find that we are so often alone. No one is sufficient unto himself, we have learned as the years have gone on. The song that says, "I'm going to sit right down and write myself a letter," is expressive of the pathetic result of trying to supply TLC for ourselves.

Our person outside may be valiant and pretend that everything is all right, but inwardly that person is wondering: "Does anybody care?" There is a completely satisfying answer to that sad question—God cares.

In fact the evidences that God cares are strewn so lavishly around creation that it is strange that we get so downhearted and indulge in so much self-pity. As we can read in the New Testament, God knew when he made us what our needs would be: God never forgets the essentials necessary for the person outside and has constructed the world and the universe to provide the most generous care for man.

Rufus Jones, the Quaker writer, marveled at what he called "God's surplus." Man needs a sunset at close of day, but does he need the gorgeous spectacle of beauty to be seen when the sun goes down? We have two lungs, two kidneys, two eyes when we could get along quite well with one of each. Seeds planted for food do not simply reproduce themselves, but multiply forty, sixty, a hundredfold. Under the earth are great treasures of minerals and fuels. And who knows what the next generation may find stored away in outer space for the future care of our "exploding population."

Beyond all of this, however, is the much more comforting knowledge that each of us can be sure that his outside person is under the eye of God. More than the birds, more than the flowers of the field, more than the stars in the sky, the individual is known and loved by the Heavenly Father.

Finding tender, loving care: I Pet. 5:6-7.

Prayer: Sometimes I forget in my desperation, O Lord, that thou dost care for me; may I be ever aware of thy kindness. Amen.

Sheltered

"I will abide in thy tabernacle for ever: I will trust in the covert of thy wings." (Ps. 61:4)

Admiral Richard E. Byrd, in his book *Alone*, tells of a day during one of his Antarctic explorations when he climbed the ladder from his underground cabin to get some fresh air and exercise and to take some scientific observations. When he was ready to return to the warmth of the buried room, he could not find the trapdoor! He shares with us the dreadful anxiety that was his as he searched feverishly for the small opening. He knew that he could not live long outside in the deadly cold.

This presents another truth about that person outside—shelter is as necessary as food and drink. The protection may be a house, one room in a home, warm clothing, or a temperate climate. Through the years we hunt for refuge as urgently as did Admiral Byrd. Some kind of dwelling must be had at all costs: the body is not made to endure constant exposure.

And since this is true of the person outside, God has made provisions in the forests and in the ground that wood, metal, glass, wool, and cotton might be available for fashioning into clothing and more durable shelters.

As is true of the need for food and drink, this dependency of the body for covering throws us back on the mercy of our Heavenly Father. The person outside cannot exist apart from the generous care of the Creator.

Perhaps to symbolize this peril of the person outside when exposed to the enemies of cold wind, damp blizzards, and extreme heat, the people of the Middle Ages declared their churches sanctuary for men being pursued. If the pursued could get into the holy building before being caught, their foes were not permitted to enter: God was their refuge.

Feeling this same sense of shelter, the poet Whittier, housebound by a great snowstorm wrote in "Snow-Bound":

> What matter how the night behaved?
> What matter how the north-wind raved?
> Blow high, blow low, not all its snow
> Could quench our hearth-fire's ruddy glow.

Where God is, the person outside finds protection.

God's sheltering: Ps. 91:1-6.

Prayer: Without pampering myself, O Lord, may I accept, with its meaning, my need for walls around me. And may I be grateful for the place I have. Amen.

Mind-Nourished

"He has made everything beautiful in its time; also he has put eternity into man's mind, yet so that he cannot find out what God has done from the beginning to the end." (Eccl. 3:11 RSV)

All of us have seen at one time or another a televised session of the United Nations Security Council, or of some other conference that could affect us and our world. As an important official from another country spoke in a language foreign to us—Russian, Syrian, Greek—we have been dismayed. What did he say? Is he friendly to us, or is he threatening? And then an interpreter translated and gave to us in English the meaning of the address that had been made. Then we knew what was going on.

To some extent, our mind is such an interpreter. The person inside speaks a language of the spirit, and the person outside understands only the physical. The mind is the confidant of both. Thus the mind is able to nourish the body.

Doctors have learned this truth of the mind affecting the body. Some physicians have dared estimate that 50 percent of the ills brought to them for curing have been brought on by a lack of good mind-nourishment. This may be particularly true of older people. And a magazine enjoying a large national circulation regularly runs articles insisting that the happy person has far less serious sickness than the unhappy person.

In the verse at the head of this chapter we observe that God provided beauty for the mind to contemplate, he planted in the mind the perspective of eternity, and he placed limitations to the seeking of the mind in order that it might have an exciting series of daily discoveries of the things the Lord has done. By this healthful plan for the mind, why should not the person outside receive a lovely interpretation of the words of the Creator?

As we conclude our examination of the person outside—the body—have we not found that that person has much to do with the happiness and success of the person inside? And have we not found that the person outside can share the gladness of the whole person? There appears to be no part of us that need be despised.

The responsibility of the food-giver: Matt. 24:45-47.

Prayer: I am learning, O Lord, how valuable and important is this person outside. May I use him in reverence. Amen.

*The
Person
with Persons*

Desert Island for Sale

"For none of us liveth to himself, and no man dieth to himself." (Rom. 14:7)

> FOR SALE: One Desert Island; rugged, secluded, no transportation. Reasonable terms to anyone who will sign a legal agreement to live alone on the property for a period of not less than five years.

Who would buy such an island? Who would condemn himself to five years of solitude? A week —perhaps even a few months—might seem possible and romantic as we remember Robinson Crusoe and his strange adventures. But five years! Five years without seeing the face of another human being; five years without hearing a voice other than our own; five years without the moral support of a companion! Who would freely choose such a fate?

For the fact is that the person inside and the person outside combine to make the person with persons. And this person with persons is just as real as the other two. This inquiry that we are making concerning ourselves could not be complete without recognizing the social drives that are as natural as the other hungers and thirsts that we have found in our makeup.

Our need for the company of others is as old as mankind. After God had created man, He knew (since man was in His image) that Adam could not bear to live alone. Just before Eve was formed the Creator said: "It is not good that the man should be alone; I will make him an help meet for him" (Gen. 2:18).

Proofs of our urge to have friends and acquaintances are expressed unthinkingly by young people: "How was the party? *Who was there?*" And those of us who have observed boys and girls in their homes know how busy they keep the telephone! Not that we are much different in our sixties, seventies, eighties—or if we live to be a hundren!

Improved transportation is permitting the full play of the built-in abhorrence for a desert-island existence, and men who study population movements predict that within a decade or so our country will be one vast city. Where people are, other people are drawn. Local churches, clubs, societies, senior citizens' groups attract members. Retirement colonies are preferred by many to living in rented apartments.

The person with persons calls himself, loudly, to our attention!

One who would not break with a companion: Ruth 1:15-18.

Prayer: I remember, Lord, that thou didst gather together twelve men to share thine earthly life. Give me worthy company, I pray. Amen.

Part of a Whole

"Now I beseech you, brethren, by the name of our Lord Jesus Christ, that ye all speak the same thing, and that there be no divisions among you; but that ye be perfectly joined together in the same mind and in the same judgment." (I Cor. 1:10)

"What is that on your desk?" a man asked a librarian.

The librarian picked up the object in question and turned it this way and that; then she admitted, "I really do not know what it is, I use it for a paperweight. When I visited an automobile factory the guide gave me this."

"This" was a small gear-like piece of metal with

perfectly formed teeth, or cogs, and a short shaft. As part of a whole machine it would have had a purpose and a definite place, but separated from its companion parts it could only serve to hold down a few sheets of paper.

Perhaps this sadly misplaced little casting speaks a truth about our person with persons: that person is part of a whole and cannot take his proper place in life or do his God-given task except in the company of others. Like the gear, that person is made to mesh with his fellowmen day by day as this world moves toward the purpose of the Creator.

To bring this truth into the realm of people, we may think of mankind as a great team on the field of life. But unlike the athletic teams engaged in games of baseball, football, or basketball that have squads in reserve, this team has no substitutes. Unless the person with persons is doing his share in the unfolding of history, some spot will stand unprotected, and an opening will be made for forces of evil to come through.

And there is no retirement from being a part of the whole. The person with persons may grow old in years, or may exchange an active occupation for a less active one, but he is still a vital team member.

These considerations must bring to us a sense of being needed. Since no one can take our assigned position in the world of man and no one can do the work we are set to do, how shall we say that we have passed our usefulness? We may have faith to believe that even after we have passed from this earth we continue to be part of the whole. What we have done and said, what we have been, will guarantee that there will be no sagging of that section of the lifeline we have been given to hold.

Some who accepted their part: Acts 4:32-34.

Prayer: May I look out at the world this day, O Lord, and know for sure that I am not replaceable. Amen.

In a Home

"We took sweet counsel together, and walked unto the house of God in company." (Ps. 55:14)

"Together," "in company"—what magic expressions!

And where does the person with persons find this happy condition better than in a home?

But we may say to ourselves, a person may want to be with persons and yet must occupy a room or apartment alone. What then? Why then the home is a place where others will come and, perhaps of more importance, where persons have been. Books, magazines, newspapers, letters, recorded music, a radio, a television set assure that company is always present. Like a lingering scent of perfume other persons leave behind them something for remembrance. Echoes of conversation and laughter start up unexpectedly.

Too, the place which our person with persons calls home is patterned after the great home that God has built around us. We are roofed over and walled in: the world is arched with sky and curtained by horizons. Our pantry is stocked with provisions for ourselves and a little "extra" for an unexpected guest. The world is a horn of plenty, "flowing with milk and honey." For everyone in this house there is space: in the world there are miles and miles of land waiting for dwellings. Indeed, home is symbolic of our meeting place with others. When we say, "I want to go home," could we not be expressing a longing to be where we can be with persons on an intimate basis rather than voicing a desire to be away from everyone?

If we think about it, we may be able to discern our home putting out probing tendrils that will find a lodgment and become roots to make the home secure.

Most of us probably have moved from one home

to another during the years, and we remember the helpful people who came in. Perhaps the Welcome-Wagon woman, the chaplain of the hospital, or a hostess in a retirement center came to tell us about our neighbors, about stores, about churches —depending upon our circumstances. And with these directions our shoots went out, and we became established, persons with persons again. A patient in a Massachusetts hospital was bedfast in one room for fourteen years, but she managed to make that room a home, rooted deep. Her mail, her nurses, her doctor, her visitors kept her "together . . . in company."

Each of us, as a person with persons, can agree without mawkishness with the song title, "Home, Sweet Home."

Housebound with the Lord: Ps. 84:1-5.

Prayer: Bless my home, O Heavenly Father. Amen.

Link in a Chain

"And next unto them repaired Meremoth. . . . And next unto them repaired Meshullam. . . . And next unto them repaired Zadok." (Neh. 3:4)

    The walls of Jerusalem had "come tumblin' down" during the exile of the Israelites. Enemies were about to enter through the breaches, as were wild animals. There was no time to let out a contract for the work: every part of the wall must be fixed immediately and *at the same time*. Nehemiah hit on the only possible way of doing it. He formed an endless chain of men, each of whom repaired that section of the wall in front of him.

    Our person with persons is this kind of link in a

chain of people. He does not work alone; he does not bear all of the responsibility. But the human chain is no stronger than he is as a link.

Sometimes we hear a person described as "a loner," "a lone wolf," "going his own way." If this is true of anyone he must be dragging the human chain with him inasmuch as each of us is bound in the great bundle of life in the world.

Perhaps this thought of mankind as a chain and each of us as a link will answer the question raised by us as we grow old, and asked by infirm people: "Why am I left here? Why can't I die and have it over with? I am of no use to anybody." In God's eyes these people must still be necessary to maintain the productiveness of mankind. Every piece of the wiring in a house is essential to the flow of electricity for light and power. The person with persons serves often by a word, a small deed, a prayer, a letter to pass on the message of God through humanity.

Or another illustration may help us to understand our essential work. Pipelines are laid across great wastes of desert to carry oil from the wells to the refineries. The pipe under the drifting sands is never seen and lies hidden for years, while the pipe exposed in the city where the fuel is needed is always seen and is kept shining. But if the flow of oil stops, the almost forgotten bit of pipe in the obscure and buried spot becomes of the utmost importance; money and hours are spent without reckoning to find the place where the break is. As long as we live, can we not be sure that God is still using us to deliver something needful to his children?

If we think of our relationship with others, this person with persons seems a link in a great chain.

A human chain is described: Isa. 41:1-9.

Prayer: O Father, if I can no longer initiate action, may I serve to pass on the motion of others. Amen.

Doing with Others

"Not that we lord it over your faith; we work with you for your joy, for you stand firm in your faith."
(II Cor. 1:24 RSV)

A man had the opportunity of traveling (for the first time) from New England to California. He debated with himself, should he go alone, or join with a group of others bound for the same place and event? Rather hesitantly he chose to go in the party. And he has always been glad. Things that he saw and things that he did were so much more enjoyable than if he had been by himself. In later years he thought, "How could I have seen the true beauty of the Grand Canyon except for the friends who shared with me their impressions?"

Life, also, is a trip—a trip of much larger proportions and a trip that will pass thousands of spots more important to us than a great national park. How wonderful that the person with persons can do things with others, pass through joyful or tragic events with others, begin and end days and years with others!

Doing a jigsaw puzzle is illustrative of working together. Four or five may be hunched over a table covered with hundreds of pieces. Slowly the pieces are put into place, and the design begins to take shape. Frequently a player holds an odd-sized piece of indeterminate color in his fingers and searches in vain for a matching spot. Then another player will discover an opening and suggest, "Try it there!" And sure enough, it fits! And isn't there always one person who thinks it a "waste of time" to spend hours on a puzzle? Once in awhile he circles the table to see what is going on. Then from the advantage of standing over the picture he sees an unused piece and a spot that match! From that moment he pulls up a chair and is caught up in the common excitement.

This may be a simple explanation of what happens in our world and in our culture when we are doing with others. Not only is there more fun, but there is more real achievement. Many eyes, many ears, many brains find resources to match needs far more quickly than is true when all efforts are individual.

Sometimes we are tempted to think that others are cleverer than we: Who needs the small act we can perform in the later years of life? And then we can think of a great orchestra that depends upon the man with the little triangle as well as upon the first violinist. The qualification in life is to be able to read God's music!

The encouragement of doing with others: Heb. 10:24-25.

Prayer: Open to me, O Lord, the miracle that lies in eating together, talking together, serving together. Amen.

Feelings Shared

"Rejoice with them that do rejoice, and weep with them that weep." (Rom. 12:15)

Francis of Assisi, according to the accounts of some of his biographers, bore on his body the marks of nails as did the body of Jesus. The explanation is that this preacher of the poor entered so fully into the sufferings of his Lord that he even showed the outward signs. Whether or not we accept the old reports, this is an illustration of sharing the feelings of another.

Our person with persons is at his best when he can take to himself the emotions and experiences of other people. Life becomes richer and deeper.

A minister confessed to this indebtedness when,

as he was retiring from his last church, he said, "I cannot think of a more satisfying career than that of a parish pastor. These forty years have been sheer romance." Things that had happened to him personally could never have supplied the full scope and range of living that had come from being moved by what happened to others. In forty years he had lived the equivalent, perhaps, of a thousand years. Think of the joys of all the weddings! The sorrow of the funerals. The exultation of those who had found success. The bitterness of going through failure, and knowing the frustration of such an experience. Youth, age, beauty, physical handicaps, plenty, want, passion, indifference had all paraded themselves before this man of God. The feelings of all his people had surged through his heart and mind.

But we need not be retired clergymen to know this expansion of our limited individual lives. As friends, as fellow workmen, as neighbors, as observers with compassion, all of us have shared, and can share, that which deeply moves our brothers and sisters. And how linked we then become to all mankind!

That we have a divinely given capacity for weeping and rejoicing with others is proved by the tears that come to our eyes when we read a heartbreaking story, attend a lovely wedding, watch a sad television program; and by the laughter that swells within us when someone else is laughing heartily.

There comes the time, of course, when we are shut away from firsthand knowledge of a great crowd of people but, even so, we have some whose feelings can be our feelings. Beyond this small circle we can, however, keep in touch by newspapers, letters, and reports: we need never fully withdraw into ourselves.

Read of One shared our feelings: Isa. 53:4-5.

Prayer: May I never grow so callous, Lord, that I cannot sympathize and struggle with others. Amen.

One Body

"For as the body is one, and hath many members, and all the members of that one body, being many, are one body: so also is Christ." (I Cor. 12:12)

Americans have been called the greatest "joiners" in the world. It has been said that no matter what the organization an ad in a magazine can bring in members by the score. Book clubs, record clubs, hobby clubs, fruit-of-the-month clubs prosper soon after they are announced. Societies, associations, and political groups flourish. It is a rare obituary in the paper that does not close by listing the "memberships" held by the deceased!

But are we sufficiently aware of our greatest

privilege—being a distinct part of the body of mankind? Stretched across the great expanse of the earth, this body moves, gets its food, accomplishes prodigious things, reaches out its arms to outer space, pokes into the depths of the sea, and vents its joys and angers. Of this body our person with persons has been destined of God to be a part.

Even if we would, it is not possible to sever ourselves from this body. We stand or fall with it, we survive or perish in its life or death. The future of the world is the future of the body and not of any one small portion of it.

Possibly a reflection on this position of ours will serve to dampen our urge to criticize what the body does! We could be in the spot of the man who kicks something (and hurts his own foot!) because his hands have been clumsy in handling a golf club.

This means that we cannot stand off and view the body as a stranger and appraise what it is doing badly. We are the body. And yet we older ones do grow cranky in our homes sometimes because "stupid" or "noisy" people are disturbing us. This kind of thing is expressed in the story of the boy who was unaware of echoes. He stood on a mountain and shouted, "Hello!" and he heard "Hello" in return. Excited by this experience he asked, "Who are you?" and the same question came back: "Who are you?" When his words were repeated several times he decided someone was making fun of him, and he started across the valley to find and punish the rude fellow! We may be able to train other members of the body, but can we disclaim them or get away from them?

Each body part is necessary and equal: I Cor. 12:14-26.

Prayer: Dear Father God, sometimes I wish I were a more important part of the body of thy people: give me to know how much I am needed where I am. Amen.

Hearing Together

"Now we believe, not because of thy saying: for we have heard him ourselves." (John 4:42)

There are whistles made with a pitch so high that the human ear does not register the sound, but dogs can hear, and they come running when such a whistle is blown. And the world is filled with sounds of many pitches. The person with persons hears for and with others and reports what he hears.

Often when we are sitting peacefully in the evening, someone in the room will start up and say, "Did you hear that?" We inquire, "What?" "Why I don't just know what it was." Then we all listen, and from what two or more hear the mystery of the sound is usually cleared up. If the sound is still strange we may go outdoors and ask others to listen.

The point is that each of us has a capacity for hearing unlike that of anyone else; each of us misses some sounds, and perhaps each of us hears something more distinctly than does his friend. Hearing together is for safety and for pleasure. This is especially true as we grow older and become what others who are younger casually call "Hard of hearing" or "deaf." Then as never before we profit by hearing together.

And while we are thinking of physically impaired hearing it might be well to distinguish between the outer and inner ear. Let us not think of this in a medical way but rather as the outer physical ear and the inner spiritual ear. By this standard some of the "deafest" people we know have the keenest true hearing of what goes on in the minds and hearts of men. Like the dog hearing his special sound, we have our kind of sound that is missed by others.

Indeed there are discussion groups that constantly use the expression, "I heard you saying." After a man or woman has expressed an opinion or pleaded for a line of action, each one in the group will comment on the speech as he "heard" it. All heard the same words, but each one heard a different meaning hidden in the words. By this method these groups hear together, each member reports what he hears, and they come to a decision of what the truth is.

The person with persons gains in many ways by not being separated and left to his own devices, but one of the greatest advantages of mingling with others is the privilege of hearing lovely and meaningful things and of pooling the sounds or impressions for the common good.

How things are heard differently: Mark 12:35-37.

Prayer: I have ears, Lord. May I hear. Amen.

Loneliness Unnecessary

"I, even I only, am left, . . . Yet I have left me seven thousand in Israel, all the knees which have not bowed unto Baal, and every mouth which hath not kissed him." (I Kings 19:14, 18)

The prophet Elijah had a sense of great loneliness; he thought that there was no one else who followed the one true God. But God told him that he was not alone—indeed, there were seven thousand others in Israel of like mind with him!

Perhaps loneliness is one of the worst ills of modern man. People have said that they feel most alone when surrounded by thousands of strangers in a great city. Families die off, and some of us feel with Elijah that we alone are left. A big house filled with voices must be exchanged for one room or a hospital bed. We say, "No one understands me."

And yet each of us, no matter what his situation, can be answered by God that we are not at all alone! For one thing, God is always present, and no one can be alone when he is nearby. It is as the poetess Emily Dickinson said of her father, that when he was in the room, even when he was sound asleep on the couch, the house was full!

Indeed, the fact that we have found out about ourselves that one facet of our being is a person with persons is proof that we are not destined for loneliness; that person will find persons somewhere, somehow.

Other persons people our memory when physically we are apart from society. Mental pictures of friends, acquaintances, family come back; we hear characteristic sayings or words of advice. We find company among people who have given themselves away in books or paintings.

Frequently the cure for loneliness is simply to open doors. In *Laddie* by Gene Stratton Porter an elderly, embittered man lived with his wife and daughter in a fine house, but he would admit no one other than his own. Finally, in his great loneliness he struck up a friendship with a little girl who walked by his gate. As they talked, she in childish simplicity asked why he would not "open his door"? He thought this over and decided to invite neighbors to come in. This was the answer to his problem. Sometimes we may have closed doors of pride, hurt, or shyness which the person with persons must throw open wide.

A promise of companionship: Matt. 28:16-20.

Prayer: Be thou my guest, O Lord. I have opened the door. Amen.

Lovely Mosaic

"And beside this, giving all diligence, add to your faith virtue; and to virtue knowledge; And to knowledge temperance; and to temperance patience; and to patience godliness." (II Pet. 1:5-6)

"And just to think," we say of a successful person, "he is a self-made man, he did it all for himself." We are speaking extravagantly, of course, for no one can go through the world, a person with persons, without being influenced by the people he meets.

Indeed, someone has said that everyone is a *mosaic* of every person he meets. This brings to mind a lovely design made up of scores or hundreds of pieces of colored glass, stone, or similar material. Each of the pieces, whether of drab or bright hue, is a necessary part of the completed picture.

With this in mind, we may understand better the exasperated complaint of one who thinks she has received an injury: "You wouldn't believe what she did to me!" Even that woman herself possibly does not know exactly what the other has done to her but there has been the insertion of a piece that will forever be included in her life mosaic.

Does this mean that we are too vulnerable? Should we say to our person with persons: "Go among people who have pretty, happy, bright things to place in my life mosaic"? Not at all. For one reason, our person cannot avoid touching and communicating and dealing with a great variety of men, women, boys, and girls. This is a kindness of God. For if we look with understanding eyes at a costly mosaic we shall see that pieces that of themselves are ugly and undesirable make up the background and provide contrast for the pattern that emerges. Since this is so, can we say at this mature stage of life that anyone has failed to give us something which we need for the life we are making?

On the other hand, our person with persons is giving of himself to others. Of married people it is said sometimes that after fifty years of living together the man and woman look alike! No doubt there is some truth to this, inasmuch as there has been such a long period of exchanging mosaic pieces. This similarity can be noticed in tight little communities where one generation after another continues to stay fairly isolated from strangers.

Surely, we are not self-made, but we can by God's grace arrange the pieces that come to us into something worthy of our heritage.

A note about one who received a piece: II Tim. 1:3-7.

Prayer: There are fragments, Lord, that I need help in fitting into my life. May I see where pain goes. Amen.

The Person Eternal

Life Exciting, Except—

"Even in laughter the heart is sorrowful; and the end of that mirth is heaviness." (Prov. 14:13)

Thus far in our search for identity and in seeking an answer to "Who am I?" our complexity may seem overwhelming. There is the person inside, the person outside, the person with persons—and we have not finished with ourselves yet! Finally, we come to the person eternal. And in our examination of this person we should find the reason and the meaning for all that we are.

Perhaps this person, of all the four that we find in ourselves, causes us the most unrest and brings up the deepest questions. For instance, just as we find life exciting and wonderful that person eternal breaks in with "Yes, life is indeed wonderful, except—" The exception is that all of this wonder and gaiety and movement will come to an end. This knowledge gives a little soberness to every occasion.

A second look at this, however, will see a blessing in it. Have we ever done anything, been anywhere, had any experience that we would want stretched out through all eternity? Teachers speak of a child's "attention span" and mean that the younger the individual, the shorter the time he can concentrate on the same thing. As we grow older we can stick to one thing much longer than when we were preschool age, but is our attention span without an end? The person eternal reminds us that we are to look at life consisting of threescore and ten or fourscore years as tremendously exciting but not unchanging. This may be illustrated by the motion picture that was made by an experimental group. They trained their camera on the Empire State Building in New York and let the film roll for eight hours. When the picture was done, the viewers saw people walk in and out of the building, saw windows being raised and lowered (or at least the blinds were), and saw faces appearing and disappearing. This went on and on until the people in the theater could stand it no longer. A short inspection of the building was exciting, but eight hours!

The person eternal knows this about all that this life brings, although at the time we may think we have found something perfect: "I could look at this forever"; "This is so good I am never going to stop eating"; "What a voice! I could listen to him for years and years and years!"

Life is all the more exciting because of *except*— and we who have seen so much of life begin to realize this.

People in transit: Heb. 11:13-16.

Prayer: In all that I find, dear Lord, may I see a glimmering of the better which is to come. Amen.

"I Am Fine"

"Persecuted, but not forsaken; cast down, but not destroyed." (II Cor. 4:9)

"I have a patient," said a doctor, "who is the most exasperating man I know. When I get him on the examining table and ask him how he feels he says, "I am fine." He has a serious condition and he knows it, but he is 'fine'!"

What the physician did not realize was that he and the ailing man were talking about different persons: The doctor was thinking of the person outside while the patient was referring to the person eternal.

John Quincy Adams, the sixth president of the

United States, expressed this difference very well. A story has come down to us reporting that when Mr. Adams was eighty someone asked him how he was? He replied that the house he lived in was getting dilapidated and he found it trembling in every wind—in fact he might have to move out soon—but as for John Quincy Adams himself, he was very well!

This matter of true perspective is much like the view from an airplane as compared to the view from the ground. Flying a mile or two above the earth the contours of the land can be seen, and the mountains and valleys appear in their proper relationship. Cars and factories are like toys. Men are tiny moving figures. The person eternal is above all this. While we walk on the earth, however, men and cars and factories seem of the first importance, and mountains and great hills tower above us; this is the environment of the person outside. Perhaps the doctor's irritating patient was speaking from the vantage point of the eternal.

In times of great distress, of illness, of bereavement there is immense comfort in remembering that we are also the person eternal, who can be "fine" through all the desperate things life may bring. Now, in age, this must be a constant consideration. No matter what the years may do to, or take from, the person outside, the person inside, or the person with persons, the person eternal can find himself in excellent youth and health.

Another reason for what the physician may have thought to be silly optimism on his patient's part is the outlook which God gives us. Travelers on great highways that are as yet unfinished are confronted with signs: "Be prepared to exit, road ends ten miles ahead," then, "five miles ahead," then, "exit here." Contrasted to this there are signs on a certain state highway marking the distance to a town named "Future." As the miles go by, that sign continues to appear: "Future ahead," "Future ahead." We are fine because we are not obliged to "exit"; we are traveling to a sure future.

The indestructible soul: Matt. 10:28-31.

Prayer: May I face life with joy this day, O Lord. Amen.

"If a Man Die"

"If a man die, shall he live again? all the days of my appointed time will I wait, till my change come." (Job 14:14)

At one time there was a program on television called "What's Your Question?" Viewers had the privilege of submitting suggestions of things that needed answers. If you or I should be asked to name the one question above all others that calls for an answer at this point in life would it not be the question of Job: "If a man die, shall he live again?"

This is of the first importance to us because everything we have done or may do has meaning chiefly in reference to our ultimate destiny. An illustration of this is found in something that happened during the economic depression of the early thirties. The powers in Washington planned work programs to give employment to many who had no jobs. Under the Public Works Administration, projects of value to the country, such as parks, highways, and bridges, were undertaken. But there were some slipups. At least one bridge was built without access or egress roads and ramps. The bridge stood without purpose; it did not help people in their journeys. If the person eternal is not really eternal, our life's work could be equally futile.

Indeed, it is the person eternal that witnesses to unending life. Somewhere in the writings of Ralph Waldo Emerson is the story of two American senators who spent a great part of their leisure time for twenty-five years trying to find some proof of immortality. Emerson's conclusion was that the men's concern was their best proof of everlasting life. So with us. The part of us we call the person eternal is assurance of continuing existence.

Sometimes we utilize our leisure by standing

and watching construction workers putting up a new building. We may be disappointed to see wooden forms brought and locked together. We might say, "What a miserable-looking place that is going to be; don't they realize that those planks are not durable enough for the purpose?" But then after some weeks if we return, we may see the laborers knocking down the outer walls to disclose solid cement or other material which had been poured into the forms and was now hard enough to stand without their support. We might think of this part of life as the temporary mold serving as a shaping and protection for our person eternal.

A stout affirmation of life: Ps. 118:16-20.

Prayer: O Thou who art light and life, may I rest in the knowledge that I am of eternity. Amen.

What Shall We Have?

"Then answered Peter and said unto him, Behold, we have forsaken all, and followed thee; what shall we have therefore?" (Matt. 19:27)

Vacations and trips have brought us all to making the decision, "What shall we take?" If we are on the way to the seashore we shall need beach attire, sunglasses, perhaps suntan lotion and a floppy hat. If to the mountains warm clothing, stout shoes, perhaps a remedy for poison ivy! We must match our baggage to the place we're going and the period of time to be spent away from home.

However, we cannot provide the person eternal with equipment as we can the person outside. We face a situation more like the man or woman about to be inducted for military service. Civilian clothes must be discarded at the point of reception; food selected by others will be given arbitrarily; and all other things will be in keeping with the new life. The candidate for an air force, a navy, or an army career will not say, "What shall I take?" but "What shall I have?"

The apostle Peter had a sense of this difference when he put his question to Jesus. And the answer had to be in terms of this life so it could be understood while at the same time hinting at the difference: he was assured that he would have all that this world afforded, but one hundredfold.

Is not this about the best that we can expect with our limited knowledge of the currency of eternity? It is like saying to one's grandchild or to the grandchild of a friend, "We are going to take you to see the ocean tomorrow," and the child asks, "What's an ocean?" And we might say to him that it is water like the lake at Grandfather's and he can wade in it just as he does at the lake, but it is so much water, this ocean, that he will not be able to see to the other side! True, an ocean is a bit similar to a lake, but it is so much more that nothing can be compared to it.

So we find our person eternal anticipating and wondering, "What shall I have?" To a degree, this person is unanswerable. God has not told him in detail of the glories of the life to be fulfilled. This person does rise above the mundaneness of today, but today's shapes and forms are the only patterns and descriptions he knows just now. He must measure the distance to a star in terms of "light-years." He knows only the colors seen in this world.

Looking forward with amazement: I Cor. 2:7-11.

Prayer: As was true of childhood Christmases, O Lord, I wait with eagerness for the things prepared for me. Amen.

Things Abandoned

"Let him which is on the housetop not come down to take any thing out of his house: Neither let him which is in the field return back to take his clothes." (Matt. 24:17-18)

The world and the sea are strewn with things abandoned by man.

There are moments of desperation when possessions are left behind to save life. On battlefields when one side must retreat in haste the soldiers drop all weights and run for their lives. When an airplane or ship is overloaded, goods are thrown overboard to avoid disaster. Our covered-wagon ancestors dotted the plains and deserts with household and farm utensils discarded in order to get the families to safe ground.

There are tangible things which can be seen, or dug up, or recovered from the sea. But there are abandoned things that cannot be seen. In order to do his work in a foreign field a missionary must abandon dear relationships with parents or wife or children. In order to gain an education a young person may have to surrender personal pursuits and pleasant occupations. An honest thinker must abandon old theories and superstitions to follow the truth.

As life goes on, the person eternal leaves behind beloved and familiar things and experiences in order to make ready for the great existence which beckons him. As Paul said of the athlete who was determined to win the prize, he must drop weight after weight until he is free to run the race unimpeded. The older we get, the truer this becomes in our own lives.

Naturally, there is regret on our part as we throw away things, or walk away from happy times, or deny ourselves the joy of collecting "antiques" of the material or mental realm. We grow accustomed to the objects surrounding us; we become lazily satisfied with the convictions of our fathers.

But what if the person eternal will not abandon things? He may end up as two brothers of New York City, whose sad story was told in the newspapers some years ago. The two men lived together in a large house which they filled with everything they could collect. One day they were found dead. One had been smothered under a pile of debris; the other could not move through the masses of trash to get help.

By comparison eternal life appears so much more precious than anything that we must give up.

The testimony of one who abandoned much: Phil. 3:7-8.

Prayer: Relax my grip, O Lord, on anything that keeps me back from the doorway to life. Amen.

Life—a Reward

"Then spake Jesus again unto them, saying, I am the light of the world: he that followeth me shall not walk in darkness, but shall have the light of life." (John 8:12)

"He is so alive!" we say of a person in his prime, or of a child. We watch him move with purpose and vigor, we mark the signs of health in his eyes and face, and we sense the store of energy waiting to be expended.

But this same vibrant person may happen upon an illness or accident and be taken to a hospital. As we see him lie there in bed, pale and weak and needing someone to care for his smallest necessities, we are shocked at the difference that a day has brought. Yet this person is alive although helpless.

When we think of life as God's reward for things abandoned and realize that this reward makes our person eternal, we may compare the two ways of being alive. One involves simply existing (as the person in the hospital), the other having, in Jesus' words, "life . . . abundantly." The gift makes us "so alive" forever.

One expression of this life could be the change from knowing "in part" to knowing the whole of God's wonderful works. For instance, there are approximately three and a half billion people in the world. How many do we know, even casually? By age seventy, possibly we may have had dealings with as many as fifty thousand. There are about one hundred forty countries in the world. How many does the average person visit in a lifetime? Perhaps five or ten, while he lives most of his life in one locality. Records show that there are one hundred fifty-five more or less basic languages in the world. How many do we speak or read? One, two, or three? As to stars, astronomers are not ready to give an exact count; one estimate is from one hundred to two hundred billion in our galaxy alone. How many stars do we know by sight? The Big and Little Dippers, the North Star, a few of the planets?

And if we add to the list of people and objects unfamiliar to us the plants, animals, books, works of art that we have not examined or read or seen, why, indeed, we know "in part."

If the reward of abundant life is expressed in coming to know wholly what God has done, what a glorious prospect lies ahead for our person eternal! And this is just one speculation of what the light of life could mean!

The contrast: I Cor. 13:11-13.

Prayer: Lord, may I ever be amazed at the marvels of man and the world and anticipate knowing in full. Amen.

Safe in God's Hands

"My sheep hear my voice, and I know them, and they follow me: And I give unto them eternal life; and they shall never perish, neither shall any man pluck them out of my hand." (John 10:27-28)

Some years ago we were accustomed to seeing signs on large buildings reading "air raid shelter" with an arrow pointing to a basement entrance. More recently these posters were changed to "fallout shelter." The idea behind these notices is the same in each instance: Here is a place to find safety if things destructive begin to fall from the sky. But would we be completely secure if we did huddle together in underground rooms?

Our person eternal needs and has a refuge far better than anything earth can provide: he is safe in God's hands. This place of retreat is not a comparative but an absolute protection. It is guaranteed not only for things falling from above, but for all dangers that beset the soul.

Depending upon the hands of God means that we are saved by a shelter that is portable. There is no chance of our being caught out in a deadly rain or in the path of a life hurricane or tornado: the hands of God encircle us no matter where our destinies take us.

The men who sailed with Columbus might have been much happier had they believed and accepted God's offer of gathering them in his hands. The sailors had a great fear of going beyond where God watched over men and of falling off the edge of the earth into a terrible abyss of nothingness. Could this be the same kind of dread we have when we allow ourselves to sink into a state of awful depression and fear and a sense of guilt? We may be forgetting that we are safe in God's hands no matter what may befall.

That we need to remember this happy condition

of our person eternal is indicated by statistics that show how inclined we are in our later years to depend upon drugs—especially tranquilizers—to give us a sense of well-being. Do we stop often enough to imagine what the "hands of God" imply?

A homely definition is found in the Negro spiritual, "He's Got the Whole World in His Hands." Not only is God here, but he is also on the side we know as the "enemy." There can be no surprise attack against God and his people. He made all things, he knows all things, he brings purpose out of all things. This body is fading, but the person eternal can never be injured.

Choosing God's hands: II Sam. 24:13-14.

Prayer: I am guilty, O Father, of understanding thy care. Strengthen me in thy hands forever. Amen.

The Heavenly Bank

"But lay up for yourselves treasure in heaven, where neither moth nor rust doth corrupt, and where thieves do not break through nor steal." (Matt. 6:20)

 Many churches, schools, and hospitals are flimsy buildings compared to the main offices of our great banks. Perhaps the difference is that banks have treasure stored that they want to protect from robbers, while churches, schools, and hospitals have intangible treasure to give away.
 But no matter how thick the bank walls, how massive the vaults, how intricate the time locks, how clever the burglar alarms, thieves regularly

break through and steal. What shall we do with our treasure, then?

The eternal person, with so much of value for his future, can find a heavenly bank where criminals cannot get in and where deterioration is impossible. The deposits are made in a strange way.

God has his "bank tellers" moving among men to receive the treasure for safe transmission to the eternal countinghouse. We know these messengers because they come to us as people in need of this world's goods and representing good causes. As the eternal person gives of his possessions to these representatives of the heavenly bank he can be sure that the deposit is made immediately.

This is something like an insurance policy. As soon as the application is signed and approved the agent says, "You are covered from this minute. If your house burns down before you get home, you can collect the amount of the policy."

As an illustration: The Good Samaritan in the parable deposited his treasure in the heavenly bank the very minute he bound up the wounds of the injured stranger by the wayside; for him this unfortunate man was God's bank teller.

Just one thing is missing as we deal with the heavenly bank; we never receive a deposit slip, and we never know how much we have in our account. We can only follow instructions and keep on putting our treasures of money, love, prayer, and concern where God directs as we move through life.

We know, too, that the eternal person has just as much need for saving against his future as our more material person has to save for his "rainy day." Our eternal person may be a spiritual millionaire by having preferred the heavenly bank to all others through the long years.

Instructions for depositing in the bank: Matt. 19: 16-22.

Prayer: Help me see, Lord, that out of what the world calls my "necessity" I can give to save. Amen.

Life—the First Qualification

"And whosoever liveth and believeth in me shall never die. Believest thou this?" (John 11:26)

When we place a seed in the ground or in some soil in a window-box, or when we plant a flower bulb that has spent the winter in a dark basement we hope for results. Carefully we bury the seed or bulb to the right depth, cautiously we sprinkle on just enough water, and perhaps we add something to enrich the earth. And then we watch. When will we see a response from what we have planted? When will a tiny bit of green appear above the surface?

Unless there was life in the seed or bulb when

we covered it, all of our care and "green-thumb" skills will not produce a growing plant. Life is the first qualification for more life and fruitfulness.

This is true also of our person eternal; there must be life before God grants never-ending life. A writer reporting the death of an only son who had not yet been married describes how the father looked at the body of the young man and realized that there was nothing left "to build on." His family name was cut off.

Only life begets life. We notice this fact often in the accounts of the miracles of Jesus. The Lord looked for faith: "Do you believe?" "Have you any faith?" Life in our eternal person is in the form of a reaching faith that gives God something to "build on."

Happily for us that spark of life-faith is not rigidly measured to see if it conforms to a minimum standard. We have been told that faith as small as a mustard seed can be sufficient as a foundation. Just as a doctor in a hospital needs to hear only a faint heartbeat or feel the feeblest of pulses to throw all of his skill and the resources around him into the fight to extend life, so God deals with the person eternal when there is any belief in him at all.

What comfort this can bring to us! There is no effort required such as "pulling ourselves up by our bootstraps." We could not succeed in any case; we have been told (and by this time of life we know) that by our thinking or struggling we could not change our height or life-span.

In Rome there is a painting of the newly created Adam with his finger barely touching the finger of God. Thus life is flooding within him. Our person eternal need only stretch out the finger of faith.

The source of our life: Col. 3:1-4.

Prayer: I believe, Lord, help thou my unbelief. Teach me the secret of life and of faith. Amen.

There Is No Death

"And God shall wipe away all tears from their eyes; and there shall be no more death." (Rev. 21:4)

"Do people die with you?" some African men asked the missionary Livingstone. This question, expressed or implied, has been the cry of humanity from early times. In our day researchers have traveled to many parts of the earth to inquire as to the death rate. In some places there are few deaths from heart disease, in others not many from cancer, in others ulcers are not prevalent. However, there is death in all places.

There are a few scientists who are predicting

science's eventual victory over physical death. Wonder drugs, organ transplants, synthetic materials, freezing of the body until new advances may solve whatever trouble the dying person has are relied upon to give immortality. These hopes are vain hopes insofar as real death is concerned.

And it may be strange that we worry so much about what doctors are going to be able to do, since we have the promise of God that death will be no more.

Certain it is that death could be conquered only by life, and that is what happened at the tomb of our Lord. Death was swallowed up by life.

As we grow on in years, our interest in death becomes more immediate and real. There is no denying that, and there is no need to pretend to avoid the subject. A boy in grammar school thinks little about a home of his own, but as he comes nearer to graduation from college, he considers his future with greater frequency, for the time is close at hand. Now we face up to the "last, for which the first was made." No one wants to stay in the kindergarten of life forever; great achievements and knowledge are beyond.

Perhaps what we need to accept is the waking after sleeping. This life, with all its excitments and romance as well as its toil and suffering, seems so desirable that it is hard for us to realize that this is just a bare sampling of what eternal life is. In comparison with the glories of the new world this is like a dream existence from which we shall awake to a freshness of indescribable quality.

In any event, the term "death," as we have used it, is no more. There is no room for death: life has crowded it out. Our person eternal begins to quiver with the excitement of the coming, joyous voyage to his true native land.

The shout of victory: I Cor. 15:54-58.

Prayer: From darkness to light, from feebleness to strength, from death to life, lead me, O Lord. Amen.

Conclusions

"Who am I?"

I am a person inside, with faults and failings, with graces and glories, with longings unexplained and strange fulfillments. I am a person inside, bound with a strong cord of love to my Heavenly Father.

I am a person outside, with needs and hungers, with anxieties and imaginations, with beauty and ability. I am a person outside, walking, working, and waiting; with every care attended to by the Creator.

I am a person with persons, in crowds, in small groups, in a one-to-one fellowship; taking my part and share in a world of brothers. I am a person with persons, knowing no loneliness because the Lord is near.

I am a person eternal, questioning the future, sensing my permanency, seeing that which is invisible. I am a person eternal, for whom there is no death, and whose life is hid in Christ.

Who am I?

I am one who is of the first importance to God and the world and my fellowman.

I am one who has been placed in a situation by divine decree because I am unique and have a purpose for my being.

Because I am who I am, I shall look upon myself with respect and awe, I shall value myself; my place in the struggle line of humanity will never be empty.